A WORLD OF SUPERCARS

PAUL MASON

WAYLAND
www.waylandbooks.co.uk

First published in Great Britain in 2019 by Wayland

ISBN 978 1 5263 0964 8

Credits:

Editorial: Cheryl Lanyon and Julia Bird

Design: Rocket Design

Picture acknowledgements: Alamy: Hans Blossy: 54tr. CJM Photography: 22-23c. DPA: 4-5c. GP Library Ltd: 36c. Andrew Lloyd: 56-57c. pbpgalleries: 25cr. Nick Taylor: 53cr.Jonny White: 41t. WENN Ltd: 40-41b. Dreamstime: Swtrekker: 61b. Vanderwolf Images: 58-59. Getty Images: © Bloomberg Finance LP: 16-17c. Lamborghini: 52-53c. REX/Shutterstock: ImagineChina: 12-13c, 13br. Kobal: 7b. LAT Photographic: 12c. Shutterstock: aldorado: 55t.Ed Aldridge: 38br. AlexLMX: 8tl, 9t, 18cl, 19tl, 30cl, 31tc, 31cr, 38tl, 39t, 39cr, 48bl, 49t, 54tl, 55cr. AmorSt-Photographer: 3t, 9bc, 46-47b.Yurii Andre-ichyn: 44-45bg b. Matt Antonio: 34-35bg t.baldyrgan: 49cl.Baranov E: 7cr, 29t. Roman Belogorodnov: 7tr. Darren Brode: 36-37b. Chromatic Studio: 9br, 24-25b.chubis: front cover c. Grzrgorz Czapski: front cover tl. Dan74: 26bl, 26bc. Rick Deacon: 44-45c. dimcars: 32-33c.DongLui: 3b, 18-19b, 48c. Evannovostro: 10-11bg, 14-15bg,44-45bg. Flipser: 5tr, 14tc. fotolupa: 34-35 bg c. fotomak: 26-27bg. GOLFX: 28-29c. Christopher Halloran: 38tr. Here: 2-3 bg, 22-23 bg. Narong Chai Hlaw: 24-25 bg. Zheng Huang: 14-15 c.l viewfinder: 9tc. janniwet: 8-9bg, 18-19bg, 30-31bg, 38-38bg, 48-49bg, 54-55bg.K-Nick: 8br, 9cl.Kaikoro: 49bc.Zhao Jian Kang: 20-21 bg, 50-51bg b. Zoran Karapancev: 60-61. Kaukola Photog-raphy: 50-51c, 64. Alexander Kirch: 46c. kvsan: 39tcr. Steve Lagreca: 20-21c, 31cl, 60tc.Dimitris Leonidas: 30c. LiPing: 36-37bg.Liushengfilm: 34-35b. Sam Moores: 42-43 c.Motorama: 11tl, 19tl. Mur34: 4tr. Nadezda Murmakova: 29bl. NarongchaiHlaw: 52-53bg. nikamo: 54-55 bg b. nowuseit: 12-13bg, 42-43bg. olegbush: 35c.andre onegin: 31tr. pio3: 6b. PhuiPhotoman: front cover tr. Andreas Poertner: 55b.betto rodrigues: 34-35c. John Silver: 2t, 11c. Somchai Som: front cover bg. satit_srihin: 50-51 bg t. ssuaphotos: 16-17bg, 56-57bg.StudioBKK: 8tc. Hennadi Tantsiura: 21tl. 3DMI: 39tcl. tishomir: 10tl, 26cl. Gale Uchel: 49tr. Petr Vaclavek: 39br, 40-41bg, 46-47bg. VanderWolf Images: 8bc, 10-11b.viewfinder: 29br.Miro Vrlilk Photography: 15tr. Cedric Weber: 35tr. Who is Danny: 28-29 bg. withGod: 8bl, 9cr, 18bl, 19br, 30bl, 31b., 38bl, 39bc, 48bl, 49br, 54bl. yousang: 1. Aleksandr Zavatskiy: 42cl.

Every effort has been made to clear copyright. Should there be any inadvertent omission, please apply to the publisher for rectification.

Printed in Dubai

Wayland
An imprint of
Hachette Children's Group
Carmelite House
50 Victoria Embankment
London EC4Y 0DZ

An Hachette UK Company
www.hachette.co.uk

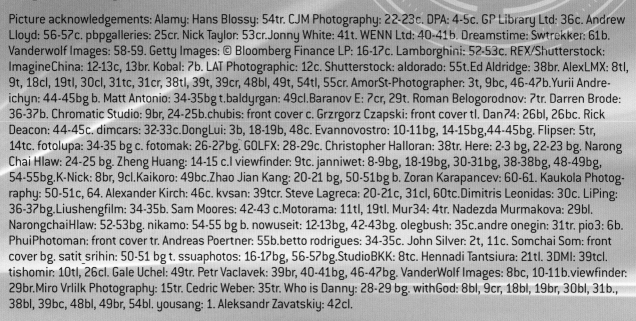

CONTENTS

JUST WHAT IS

The truth is, no one really knows what makes a car a supercar. Over 50 years after the first supercar was – possibly – produced (not everyone agrees on that, either), there still isn't a definition.

What IS true is that all supercars share at least some of the qualities shown here ...

COST

Supercars always cost either a lot of money – or a HUGE amount of money. A 'cheap' supercar like the Lotus Exige on page 40 costs £63,000 new – that's about the same as five Ford Fiestas. A really expensive supercar like the Lamborghini Veneno costs roughly £3 million, which is enough to buy several large houses.

TECH

Supercars always use the latest technology. Sometimes it's used to make the cars go faster; other times it makes them better to drive, gives them more grip, or just makes them more comfortable.

A Lamborghini Veneno like this one will set you back a cool £3 million!

A SUPERCAR?

RARITY

The manufacturers only ever make a few of each model of supercar. Sometimes it's just a handful: Pagani, for example, only made 20 Huayra BCs (see page 42). There will only ever be 500 Ferrari LaFerraris (page 14), as the company is not making any more. This rarity is why the first-ever used LaFerrari to go on sale cost twice as much as a new one.

> " Supercars are ... built to look good and to sound good and to make the owner look rich. "
>
> Jeremy Clarkson

SPEED

All supercars are fast. There are two important numbers in the Land of the Supercar: top speed and the time it takes to accelerate from 0–100 km. Really fast, really high-tech, super-expensive supercars are sometimes called hypercars.

Very few supercars are good for doing the shopping, taking the kids to school, going camping, or doing anything much except

... **GOING FAST AND SHOWING OFF** .

THE FIRST SUPERCAR?

Lots of the world's top supercar makers – Lamborghini, Ferrari and Pagani, for example – are Italian. So it's no surprise that the world's first supercar was built in Italy.

... OR WAS IT?

THE LAMBORGHINI MIURA

Before it made the Miura, Lamborghini was most famous for making tractors. One story says that Ferruccio Lamborghini, the company's owner, got so tired of his Ferrari breaking down that he decided to build his own sports car. Another says that his three top engineers worked on the Miura in secret before surprising Ferruccio with the design.

1966 SUPERCAR

Many people think the Lamborghini Miura was the world's first supercar. When it appeared in 1966, it was the fastest production car. (To be called a production car, at least 30 must have been sold.) It cost about the same as £120,000 in today's money. In 2015, a Miura sold for £2 million.

OTHER FIRST SUPERCARS

Not everyone agrees that the Miura was the first supercar. Ferrari built the 125 S as long ago as 1947. Its design was based on a racing car and had its engine in front, although it was rear-wheel drive. In 1954, Mercedes Benz produced one of the most famous cars ever: the SL300 Gullwing. Mercedes made 1,400 of them, but only 29 all-aluminium special editions. Today these are worth over £2 million.

Ferrari 125 S

Mercedes SL300

REAR-MID ENGINE

The Miura shared design features with many later supercars. The engine was rear-mid mounted and it was rear-wheel drive. It only had two seats and, unusually, it also had a spare wheel.

SUPERCAR ★ SUPERSTAR

CAR: Deusenberg Model SSJ

Movie-star owners: Gary Cooper, Clark Gable

Could the first supercar have been American? In 1935, Deusenberg released the SSJ. It was very powerful and only two were made. They were driven by the US movie stars Gary Cooper and Clark Gable, who raced them around the Hollywood Hills.

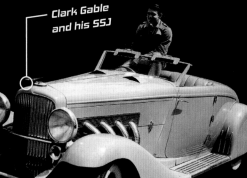
Clark Gable and his SSJ

ENGINES

Supercar fans get very excited about engine power, but also about configuration. This is how the engine's cylinders are laid out. A car's cylinders can be in a flat six, V8, V10 or V12 layout. Many drivers have a favourite configuration.

SUCK

SQUEEZE

BANG

BLOW

Fuel/air mixture sucked in

Mixture is compressed (squashed into a smaller space) as piston rises

Mixture explodes, forcing piston down, turning crankshaft

Crankshaft keeps turning, expelling exhaust gases

An engine's cylinders are chambers where a piston is forced up and down by exploding fuel. This movement turns a crankshaft, which powers the car. The volume of all the cylinders in cubic centimetres (cc) is a way of measuring the engine's size.

1 FLAT FORMATION

A 'flat' engine formation is where the cylinders are laid out in pairs. Each cylinder sticks straight out to the side of the crankshaft, opposite another cylinder. The most famous supercar maker using this formation is Porsche.

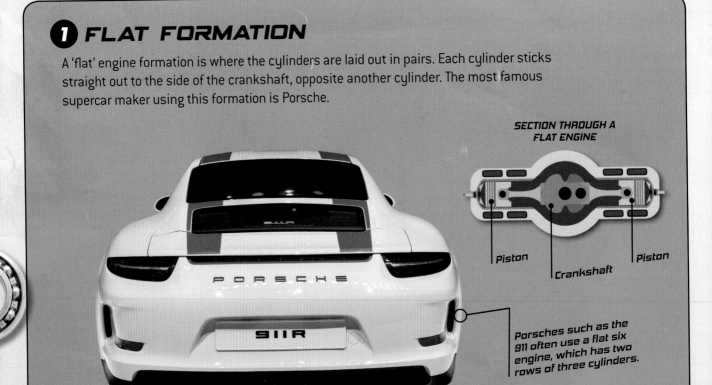

PORSCHE

911R

SECTION THROUGH A FLAT ENGINE

Piston

Crankshaft

Piston

Porsches such as the 911 often use a flat six engine, which has two rows of three cylinders.

2 V FORMATION

This is the most popular engine formation for supercars. The cylinders are in pairs, sticking up either side of the crankshaft in a V shape (seen from the front).

V-formation engines usually come in either V8, like in the McLaren 650S, V10 or V12. The numbers tell you how many cylinders the engine has. The roaring of a big V12 engine makes every supercar fan's hair stand on end.

McLaren 650S

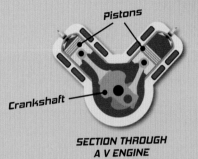

Pistons

Crankshaft

SECTION THROUGH A V ENGINE

A V formation is often used by Ferrari, Lamborghini, Pagani, McLaren and others.

ENGINE POSITIONS

An engine's position is where it is fixed to the car. Engines can be front-, mid- or rear-mounted. Normal cars have front-mounted engines, out in front of the driver.

Many supercars have rear- or mid-mounted engines. Putting the engine in the middle means its weight is balanced between the four wheels, giving better grip and handling (see page 30). Rear-mounted engines, with weight over the back wheels, usually mean a car can slow down more quickly.

Lamborghini uses a mid-mounted engine in cars such as this Aventador.

> Lamborghini's V12 … a spine-chilling soundtrack and almost lighter-than-air performance.
> Andrew English

FERRARI 812 SUPERFAST

Supercars use a lot of petrol, so they produce a lot of pollution. Because of this, few cars are still made with the biggest engines – giant V12s like the one in the 812 Superfast.

TORQUE

The torque – how hard the car drives forward, pressing you into the back of your seat – is 718 Nm (Newton metres are the units used to measure torque). That's about seven times as much as a Fiesta's.

POWER

The 812 Superfast uses the most powerful engine Ferrari has ever made. It has 588 kW (kilowatts: 1 kW = 1,000 watts) of power, so it would win a tug-of-war against 10 Ford Fiestas.

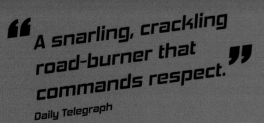
SPEED

If the driver presses hard on the accelerator pedal, the car will be doing 100 kph 2.9 seconds later. In another 5 seconds it will be doing 200 kph. Not long after that, the 812 Superfast will reach its top speed: 340 kph.

TECH TOPIC:

ASPIRATION

Aspiration is the word for how a car's engine gets air. (It needs the oxygen in air to burn fuel.) There are three main ways:

A powerful, naturally aspirated Ferrari V12 engine.

⚙ **NATURAL ASPIRATION** (which the 812 Superfast has) uses air that flows into the engine through a pipe called an inlet manifold. Air and fuel are pulled into each cylinder by a vacuum created when the piston travels downward.

⚙ **TURBOCHARGING** forces air into the engine using a turbine, which is powered by the flow of exhaust gases. Because more air gets into the engine, more fuel can be added too, producing more power.

⚙ **SUPERCHARGING** works like turbocharging, but the turbine is powered by the engine itself.

McLaren SENNA

The McLaren Senna is a racing car you can drive on the road. It's named after Ayrton Senna, McLaren's greatest Formula 1 driver. It is the lightest, most powerful, most technologically advanced McLaren ever.

RACING CAR ★ SUPERSTAR

NAME: Ayrton Senna

MOVIE: Senna

If you want to understand why racers such as Lewis Hamilton are such big fans of Senna, this is the film to watch. It tells the story of Senna's Formula 1 racing career, his struggles with rival French driver Alain Prost and his tragic death in a racing accident.

TWIN-TURBO POWER

The Senna's engine has two turbochargers. Air is channelled to the engine from a snorkel that lies flat against the back of the roof. As speed increases, the flow of air and exhaust gases drives the turbochargers and quickly spins the engine up to maximum power.

SPECIAL EXHAUST

The Senna's exhaust is made of inconel and titanium: these are rare metals that are strong, light and resist heat. The exhaust takes waste gases from the engine and pushes them out at an angle, giving the car extra grip.

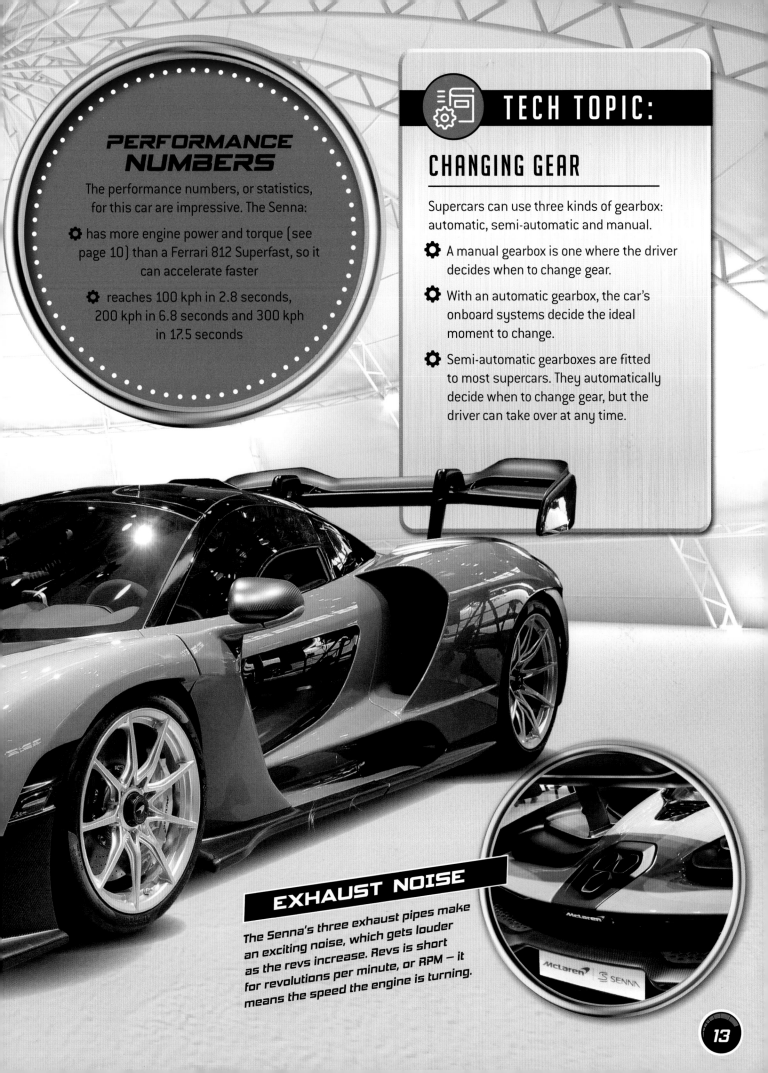

PERFORMANCE NUMBERS

The performance numbers, or statistics, for this car are impressive. The Senna:

⚙ has more engine power and torque (see page 10) than a Ferrari 812 Superfast, so it can accelerate faster

⚙ reaches 100 kph in 2.8 seconds, 200 kph in 6.8 seconds and 300 kph in 17.5 seconds

TECH TOPIC:

CHANGING GEAR

Supercars can use three kinds of gearbox: automatic, semi-automatic and manual.

⚙ A manual gearbox is one where the driver decides when to change gear.

⚙ With an automatic gearbox, the car's onboard systems decide the ideal moment to change.

⚙ Semi-automatic gearboxes are fitted to most supercars. They automatically decide when to change gear, but the driver can take over at any time.

EXHAUST NOISE

The Senna's three exhaust pipes make an exciting noise, which gets louder as the revs increase. Revs is short for revolutions per minute, or RPM – it means the speed the engine is turning.

FERRARI
LaFERRARI APERTA

What do you get when you take the 6262 cc engine capacity of a Ferrari F12 Berlinetta, add a 120 kW electric motor and remove the roof? You get a supercar to blow your mind!

THE LaFERRARI

The Aperta is based on a car called simply LaFerrari. The LaFerrari uses technology from Ferrari's Formula 1 cars. When the driver brakes, some of the braking force is stored as electrical energy. This can be used later to power the electrical motor. So, if the car's 6262 cc petrol engine isn't enough, you can get even more power.

HYBRID POWER

The Aperta's hybrid power makes it incredibly fast. The petrol engine is as powerful as a McLaren Senna's. The electric motor can add 120 kW more power – as much as a basic BMW 3-series car.

SPEED

The Aperta can reach 100 kph in under 3 seconds and 300 kph in under 15. Definitely fast enough to mess up your hairstyle!

Targa-style roof

Alfa Romeo 4C Spider with targa roof

TECH TOPIC:

TARGA, CABRIOLET OR SPYDER

Open-topped versions of supercars have different names depending on how they work.

⚙ A targa has a section of roof that can be removed. There's a roll bar and rear window behind the driver and passenger. The roll bar protects the heads of people in the car if it rolls over.

⚙ A convertible's roof folds right back, with nothing behind the driver and passenger.

⚙ Convertibles are sometimes called cabriolets or roadsters.

⚙ Both kinds of roof are sometimes called spyders or spiders.

RARE APERTA

Only 500 LaFerraris were ever made. So many people wanted one that when the first used LaFerrari appeared, its price had gone from £900,000 new to £2 million. No wonder Ferrari decided to make an open-topped version (*aperta* is Italian for 'open'). But they only built 210 Apertas and the last one sold for £7.5 million.

NIO EP9

There aren't many supercars from China, and you may never have heard of this one. NIO is a car manufacturer founded in 2014 and based in China. It has produced the amazing EP9. What's even more unusual is that the EP9 is powered by electricity, not petrol.

ELECTRIC ON TRACK

The NIO was developed using technology from a Formula E racing car (Formula E is for electric cars only), and it shows. The car has set lap records at some of the world's most famous racetracks. On some it's not only faster than other electric cars, but also petrol-fuelled supercars.

⚙ At the Nürburgring (see page 54) the EP9 once held the lap record for a production car. Its time around one of the world's most difficult circuits was 06:45.90 – less than a second slower than the new record-holder, a Lamborghini Aventador SVJ.

⚙ The EP9 also holds records at the Circuit Paul Rickard in France and the Circuit of the Americas in Texas, USA.

FOUR-WHEEL DRIVE

Each wheel is driven by its own power unit and has its own gearbox. Because of this the EP9 grips extremely well when accelerating. Specially designed wheels and tyres add more grip. The custom-built brakes, also made specially for the EP9, slow down all four wheels.

> **"** *Completely bonkers! I've been in a lot of fast cars, but the EP9 is definitely the fastest.* **"**
>
> Nicki Shields

SUPERCAR ★ SUPERSTAR

CAR: NIO EP9   **VIDEO:** Nürburgring record lap

To see exactly what a record-breaking lap of the Nürburgring looks like, head to NIO's website: **https://www.nio.io/ep9**. You can click through to an on-board video of the 06:45.90 lap (watch out for a scary moment at about 1:36). There's also a video of the EP9's self-driving lap at the Circuit of the Americas.

SELF-DRIVING SUPERCAR

At the Circuit of the Americas, the EP9 holds two track records. The first is a time with a driver of 2:11.30. The second is for a self-driving car with no driver, with a time of 2:40.33 and a top speed of 257 kph.

MASSIVE POWER

The EP9 has four electric batteries. Together they produce 1,000 kW (or 1 megawatt) of power. The car can reach 100 kph in 2.7 seconds and 200 kph in 7.1 seconds. Its top speed is 313 kph.

AERODYNAMICS

Aerodynamics is the science of how air flows around solid objects. It has a big effect on how fast a car goes and how much grip it has. Supercars often use the same aerodynamics as racing cars.

When they're thinking about aerodynamics, supercar designers have to balance two things: speed and grip.

GRIP V. SPEED

A design that channels air in a way that forces the tyres down onto the road has good grip, but is slowed down by drag. Drag is a slowing-down force caused by the car pushing against the air in front of it.

A design that slips through the air, instead of channelling it, will be faster because it experiences less drag. But a car that slips through the air will also have less grip.

That's why supercars such as the McLaren P1 (see below) have aerodynamics you can adjust at the touch of a button when you want more grip or more speed.

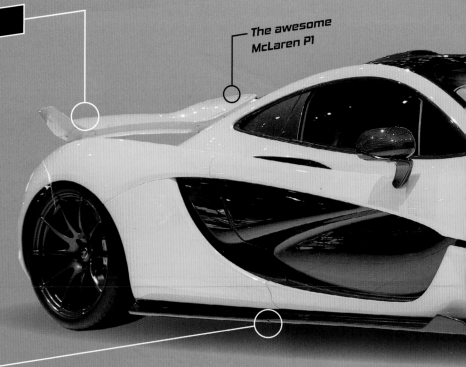

The awesome McLaren P1

REAR WING

The rear wing channels air to create downforce (see top right). This presses the rear of the car down and gives the tyres more grip. For straight-line speed the P1 has a DRS (Drag Reduction System) button. This moves the wing angle to produce less grip and more speed.

AIR FLOW

The front, sides, roof and even the floor of the P1 are shaped to improve its aerodynamics.

TECH TOPIC: DOWNFORCE

Downforce is the name for air flow that pushes the car down onto the ground. It works in the same way as the force of lift, which makes aeroplanes fly, but in the opposite direction. Downforce and lift are both created when air moves past a solid at different speeds.

Air flows more slowly along shorter top of wing

HIGHER PRESSURE ZONE

WING SECTION

Air split by front edge of wing

LOWER PRESSURE ZONE

Air flows faster along longer bottom of wing

Pressure difference causes a downward force

In Race mode, the McLaren P1's front and rear wings can create a downforce of 800 kg. That's like having one-and-a-half grizzly bears sitting on the roof.

RIDE HEIGHT

A control in the cabin puts the P1 into different settings. Choosing Race mode lowers the car 50 mm closer to the road for better aerodynamic grip. Its suspension (see page 30) also becomes 300 per cent stiffer and the way the engine reacts changes.

SPLITTER

A splitter sits below the front bumper. It helps push more air over the car and less air under it. This keeps the pressure higher above the car and presses it harder onto the road, giving more grip.

FALCON F7

The F7 wouldn't look out of place beside a line-up of Lamborghinis, Ferraris and Paganis. So it might surprise you to find out that this supercar is designed and made in the USA's 'Motor City': Detroit.

HIGH POWER

The F7's engine is extremely powerful. For real speed freaks there's a twin-turbo version of the 6200 cc motor. It produces 821 kW and rockets the car to 100 kph in 2.8 seconds. Top speed is over 320 kph.

US PERFORMANCE CARS

The USA is a huge country, with long distances between cities. Because of this, many American roads are long and straight. Straight roads are perfect for driving fast, so in the past US performance cars often focused on speed rather than going around corners quickly (part of 'handling' – see page 30). Now, though, cars such as the Falcon F7 are being designed with both high speed and excellent handling.

SIDE DUCTS

The side ducts, or openings, in front of the rear wheels suck in air to help cool the brakes and rear-mounted engine. They also channel air to improve the aerodynamics.

When liquids or gases (fluids) flow through a narrow space, two things happen:

⚙ The speed at which the fluid is moving increases.

⚙ The amount of pressure decreases.

This is known as the Venturi Effect – and for the designers of fast cars, the Venturi Effect is important. They can design the floor of the car so that air is forced into a narrower gap between the floor and the ground. This speeds up the air flow and lowers the air pressure. The lower air pressure sucks the car down towards the ground, giving it extra grip.

Air flows faster and at lower pressure under the car

FRONT AIR INTAKE

The F7 has a huge air intake at the front, which channels air under the car and helps cool the engine. The intake's lower edge acts as an air splitter, adding grip (see Aerodynamics on page 18). The car's bonnet scoops also channel air.

APOLLO
INTENSA EMOZIONE

Apollo once had a car with one of the best names ever: the 'Enraged'. Compared to that, Intensa Emozione (Italian for 'intense emotion') sounds a bit feeble. This is not a feeble car, though.

RACING-CAR DESIGN

The Intensa Emozione, or IE, is designed for the racetrack. One look tells you that this is a seriously fast car. From the massive front splitter (see page 19) to the enormous wing at the back of the car, it is loaded with aerodynamic features. Everything helps it go round bends at extremely high speed.

MASSIVE DOWNFORCE

At 300 kph, the IE's aerodynamics can generate over 1,350 kg of downforce. As the car weighs only 1,250 kg, in theory it could drive upside-down on a ceiling (as long as the driver weighed 99 kg or less so the total weight was under 1,350 kg). No one has ever actually tried this.

PERSONAL FITTING

Each IE is made to fit the person who buys it. This car doesn't have traditional seats. Instead the car's monocoque shell (see page 39) is seat-shaped inside. Padding and cushions, shaped to fit the customer exactly, are added to this. The positions of the steering wheel and the control pedals are also adjusted to fit the owner.

MASSIVE SPEED

The IE has a huge 6300 cc V12 engine behind the driver. Because the car is very light, the powerful motor drives it forward very quickly indeed. It can reach 100 kph in 2.7 seconds and has a top speed of 335 kph.

MASSIVE COST

The IE costs at least £2.3 million (a bit over £2 million), which is a lot for a car too loud to be driven legally on the road in some countries. But as Apollo are only making ten IEs, the price of used ones might actually go up.

ARRINERA HUSSARYA

Some countries are famous for their supercars – Italy for example. But supercars you might not know about are being made in some surprising places – such as Poland.

BROTHERLY BEGINNINGS

Poland's supercar story began when two brothers, Marek and Łukasz Tomkiewicz, decided their country should have its own supercar manufacturer. In 2008 they set up Arrinera and started to build prototype, or experimental, cars. By the start of 2016 they were ready to release their first car: the Arrinera Hussarya GT racing car.

LIMITED NUMBERS

The first Hussarya 33 appeared in 2017, and only another 32 will ever be made. All will be fitted with a 6200 cc V8 engine that produces 485 kW of power.

TEST CAR

MICHE

PPG

HILLCLIMBS

Hillclimbs are popular competitions among fans of performance cars. They are time trials, where the car that reaches the top in the fastest time is the winner.

Hillclimb courses are usually steep, narrow and twisty, so cars with good handling and acceleration normally do well. The Goodwood course is especially tricky, making the Hussarya GT's win even more impressive.

GOODWOOD RECORD

In June 2016, the Hussarya GT took part in the Goodwood Festival of Speed in the UK. It was the first Polish supercar ever to enter the Festival's famous hillclimb competition. But not only that – it WON! It was over two seconds faster than the second-placed Porsche 911 GT3 Cup.

The Hussarya GT at Goodwood.

FAMOUS NAME

The Hussarya is named after a famous Polish Army cavalry (horse) unit. In 1683 the Polish Hussars defeated Turkish troops outside the city of Vienna, Austria. The victory stopped the Ottoman Empire expanding further into Europe.

GOING ELECTRIC

Arrinera is planning to make an electric-powered version of the Hussarya.

FERRARI FXX-K EVO

The Evo (short for 'evolution') is a version of the Ferrari FXX-K. Most people thought the FXX-K was already so good it didn't need to evolve into something better.

THE XX FERRARIS

Ferraris with the letters XX in their name are part of a special test programme. The owners can drive their cars at certain tracks and events, then give Ferrari feedback on how the car's technology works. You can't ask to be a member of this test programme: Ferrari has to invite you. That might be why all 40 FXX-Ks were sold before most people had even heard of them.

Ferrari FXX-K

AERODYNAMICS

The Evo was developed using a wind tunnel to tune its aerodynamics. A wind tunnel is a tube where air moves very fast over the object being tested. The car has a fixed rear wing, a redesigned front, and air-channelling vanes all over the car, including on its underside. Overall, the Evo has 75% more downforce than a LaFerrari (see page 14).

NO ROAD, NO RACE

Although the FXX-K Evo is thought to cost £2–3 million (no one knows for sure), you can't drive it on the road, or in a race as it doesn't meet the rules. You can only drive it on a racetrack. In 2015, Ferrari said, "Road cars have homologation (legal approval) concerns, race cars have rules, these (XX Ferraris) have no barriers. We test on them what we can't on road or race cars."

> " First and second gears were a complete blur ... The V12 [engine] screaming through the bare carbon-fibre cabin is ... a sound that you can feel in your guts. "

Evo magazine

ENERGY RECOVERY

The 'K' in the FXX-K's name stands for Kinetic Energy Recovery System. Developed for Ferrari's Formula 1 team, the system uses energy from when the car brakes to charge a battery that powers the electric motor.

POWER

The Evo has two motors: a 6300 cc V12 that produces 630 kW and an electric motor that can add up to 140 kW extra. It is thought it can reach 100 kph in 2.5 seconds and has a top speed of about 350 kph (Ferrari have not released any precise data on this).

McLAREN 720S

Performance cars with funky doors have been popular since the Mercedes SL300 'Gull-wing' of 1954 (see page 7). If you want a modern supercar with funky design and a lot more performance, the 720S might be for you.

TEARDROP ROOF

The 720's teardrop-shaped roof is mostly toughened glass, supported by a carbon-fibre frame to protect people inside in a crash.

AERODYNAMIC DESIGN

The 720S has a rounded shape. Every curve is designed to reduce drag, add grip or cool the engine and brakes. Of course, the 720S has the front splitter, rear wing and special floor seen on most supercars, but McLaren didn't stop there. The headlights channel air, the doors channel air — even the wing mirrors have been designed to channel air in the best way possible.

DOOR DESIGN

The 720S has doors that extend almost to the middle of the roof. They lift forwards and up to make it as easy as possible to get in and out of the low-down car.

28

TECH TOPIC: GULL-WING DOORS

When gull-wing doors are open, they look a bit like a seagull's wings. Doors like this became famous after they appeared on the Mercedes SL300.

The SL was based on a racing car. The only way to add doors was to put the hinge in the middle of the roof, instead of in front. The doors looked so cool that they've since been used on many high-performance cars.

Mercedes SL300

OPTIONAL EXTRAS

If you don't mind adding to the basic £220,000 cost, the optional extras you can buy include carbon-fibre racing seats, and a telemetry system with a lap-time recorder and cameras that record every moment of your drive.

MCLAREN 720S V. FERRARI 488 GTB

The McLaren's closest supercar rival is the Ferrari 488 GTB. Like the 720S, the Ferrari has a 4-litre turbo-charged V8 engine and both cars have top speeds of about 330 kph. So, which would win in a race to, say, 275 kph? The McLaren, by quite a long way. In fact, the McLaren could let the Ferrari have a head-start of almost three seconds (it would be doing 100 kph by then) and STILL reach 275 kph first.

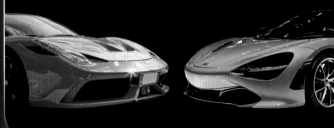

⊙ HANDLING

The word 'handling' describes what a car is like to drive through bends and over different surfaces. Aerodynamics decide the amount of grip, but many other factors also affect the car's handling.

ENGINE POSITION

Where an engine is placed in a supercar (see pages 8–9) affects where most weight is. Weight towards the back of the car gives it better braking. If the car is also rear-wheel drive it has better acceleration and is lighter. It also usually turns more quickly. That's why most supercars have rear- or mid-rear engines.

FRONT/REAR WEIGHT

Rear-engined supercars usually have a 40/60 weight distribution. This means roughly 40 per cent of their weight is on the front wheels and 60 per cent on the rear wheels.

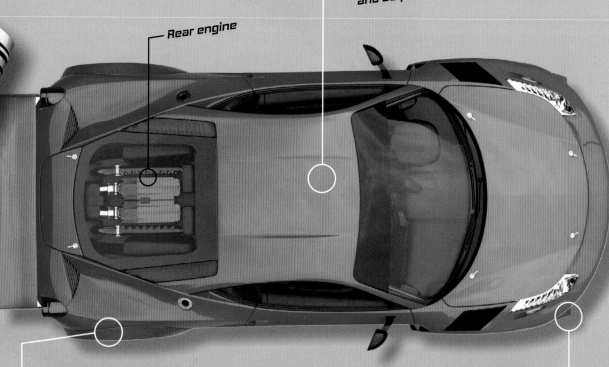

Rear engine

DRIVE

Most supercars have rear-wheel drive, so the engine's power goes to the rear wheels. Some send power to all four wheels (all-wheel or four-wheel drive), which helps the tyres grip the road better.

SUSPENSION

A car's suspension absorbs bumps in the road, making the ride more comfortable. Soft suspension absorbs bumps well, but feels wobbly at high speed. Hard suspension is less comfortable, but better at high speed and on smooth roads (or racetracks).

POWER DELIVERY

Power delivery is the way a car's engine delivers its power. When the driver pushes the accelerator, does the engine release maximum power immediately? On a racetrack this is a good thing, giving maximum acceleration. On a road, where someone could step out in front of you as you pull away, it might not be such a great idea.

On a busy street accelerating too fast can be dangerous

TECH TOPIC: DRIVER MODES

Supercars usually have onboard computers that control things like suspension and power delivery. The driver can choose different 'driver modes' to alter the settings for these (and sometimes the aerodynamics too). They have names like the Lamborghini Aventador's Strada (road), Sport (fast road) and Corsa (race) settings.

The 2015 Dodge Challenger SRT Hellcat took things further: it had two keys, a black one and a red one. Only the red one gave full power.

BUGATTI
CHIRON SPORT

The Chiron was already pretty much the fastest car you could buy, so when they made a Sport version, Bugatti kept the engine and power the same. The changes focused on making the car's handling even better.

POWERHOUSE ENGINE

The Chiron Sport has the same engine as the 'ordinary' Chiron. It's a 7993 cc W16, with four turbochargers. That's not a mistake: it really is a W-formation engine. It's basically two V8s, like the one in the McLaren 720S on pages 28–29, side-by-side. The engine develops (car language for 'produces') 1119 kW of power – so this car would win a tug-of-war against four Porsche 718 Boxsters.

CHANGED STEERING FEEL

Bugatti has changed the way power is delivered to the wheels, to give faster handling and more grip when accelerating. The Chiron Sport also responds more quickly when you move the steering wheel.

COSTS AND BENEFITS

In the world of supercars, if you have to ask how much something costs you probably shouldn't buy it. But ... the Chiron Sport costs roughly €2,650,000 (£2,350,000), which is about 10 per cent more than the Chiron. It has the same acceleration (0–100 kph in 2.5 seconds) and the same top speed (420 kph). But the Sport weighs 18 kg less, and is five seconds faster around a test track.

REDUCED WEIGHT

Overall the Chiron Sport is lighter than the Chiron. The wheels weigh less and the windscreen wipers (and some other parts) are made of carbon fibre to make them lighter – and every little bit helps!

REVISED SUSPENSION

In Handling mode, the Chiron Sport has harder suspension (see page 30) than the Chiron. The stiffness is increased by 10 per cent, which Bugatti says makes the Sport quicker than the Chiron around a test track.

ASTON MARTIN DB10

If you've seen the film Spectre, you'll know why this car is famous for its handling. In the film, James Bond's Aston Martin DB10 is chased at breakneck speed through the streets of Rome by a Jaguar C-X75.

SPECTRE PROJECT

The chase scene in *Spectre* took 17 nights to film. Bond's DB10 was based on an Aston Martin Vantage and was built especially for the movie. It does plenty of drifting (sliding round corners), driving across 45° slopes and other things the car's traction-control engineers might not originally have planned. (Traction is another word for grip.) The DB10 also shoves a little Fiat 500 to over 80 kph down a narrow cobbled street, before crashing into the River Tiber as Bond ejects through the sunroof.

POWER

In real life, the DB10's naturally aspirated (see page 11) 4700 cc V8 engine takes over four seconds to reach 100 kph. A Jaguar C-X75 only takes 2.9 seconds: it's no wonder Bond has to crash into a river to escape from it.

SUPERCAR ★ SUPERSTAR

CAR: Aston Martin DB5   **MOVIES:** several Bond movies

James Bond has always loved Aston Martin cars. His favourite has to be the classic Aston Martin DB5. He has driven a DB5 in eight movies: *Goldfinger, Thunderball, Goldeneye, Tomorrow Never Dies, The World Is Not Enough, Casino Royale, Skyfall* and *Spectre*.

HANDLING

With the engine at the front, but rear-wheel drive, the Vantage uses traction control to keep the wheels gripping the road. For *Spectre*, they must have turned the DB10's traction control off so it could slide freely while filming.

BRAKING

The car has powerful disc brakes on all four wheels. The special grooved brake discs let the brake pads grip harder than normal, slowing it down for those tight turns down Rome's side streets.

FORD GT

When the Ford GT's designers were asked the three things that were most important to them, they replied: "Lap times, lap times and lap times." This meant the GT had to handle well.

RACING BACKGROUND

Ford designed the GT to take part in the 2016 Le Mans 24-hour race in France. Fifty years earlier the Ford GT40 beat the favourite (a Ferrari 488 GTB) by a minute. Ford wanted to win Le Mans again, and they built the GT to do it. It worked: in 2016, a GT crossed the Le Mans finish line in first place.

TIGHT FIT

The designers wanted to keep the cockpit as small as possible, so the seat is fixed in position however big or small the driver is. The position of the controls is adjusted to fit him or her.

An original Ford GT40 competing in the 1966 LeMans 24-hour race.

TRACK MODE

In Track mode, the car lowers down 50 mm — which doesn't sound much, but gives the GT even more grip at speed.

POWER V. AERODYNAMICS

The GT is fitted with a 3497 cc V6 engine, which sounds small. But it does have two turbochargers, 482 kW of power and reaches 100 kph in about 3 seconds. Still, this is much less power compared to many Ferraris, McLarens and others. Ford kept the engine small as they wanted the car to be as small as possible. This allows it to slip through the air more easily.

ROAD-CAR GT

To be allowed to race at Le Mans, Ford had to build and sell 500 road-car versions of the GT. Over 7,000 people asked to buy one, so the company used a long questionnaire to decide who should be the lucky owners. Ford later decided to build another 500 GTs.

REAR WING

The wing is lifted or dropped at different speeds. When the driver brakes hard, the wing lifts up and acts as an air brake.

WEIGHT

Weight is important for supercar designers and owners. A supercar's weight affects its top speed, acceleration, handling and comfort.

SPEED V. COMFORT

The super-light Lotus Evora

SPEED

A lighter car is usually faster than a heavier car with the same engine. Supercars that will be driven short distances very quickly – around a racetrack, for example – are built to be as light as possible. The British company Lotus, which is famous for building light cars, sometimes even strips out the carpets to save weight.

The luxurious cabin of the Audi R8 V10

COMFORT

If you strip out the carpets, sound insulation and door linings the car is lighter, but not very comfortable. Some supercars are for driving long distances very quickly. They need to be more comfortable. The seats are bigger and heavier, the driver's cabin is better insulated, and the engine may be bigger and weigh more. The Audi R8 V10 Quattro and Maserati Granturismo MC Stradale are examples of high-performance cars that swap light weight for comfort.

TECH TOPIC: WHAT'S A MONOCOQUE?

The first cars were made in the same way as horse-drawn carriages. They built a strong base frame for support, then added the car parts and body on top. This was called body-on-frame construction. In the early- to mid-20th century, designers started to try a new structure, where the whole exterior shell of the car provided support. It was called a monocoque ('single shell' in French).

Body-on-frame

Mechanical and body components are fixed to the frame

Monocoque

Mechanical components will be fixed to the shell

MATERIALS

The lightest supercars have as many carbon-fibre parts as possible. Carbon fibre is very light and strong. At the heart of the car is a monocoque. To this are added front and rear sub-frames, which hold the wheels, brakes, engine and other parts.

Carbon fibre is very expensive. Some supercar makers use steel or aluminium to keep costs down. These add weight, but that's not always a bad thing. For example, when the Dutch company Vencer built a supercar for long-distance travel, it combined a metal frame with carbon-fibre body panels. The Vencer Sarthe feels like a racing car, but is comfortable enough to drive across Europe.

TECH TOPIC: CARBON FIBRE

Carbon fibre is made of at least two things: carbon-fibre cloth and resin. Car parts start life as carbon-fibre cloth. The cloth is laid out in the shape that's needed, perhaps by laying it over a form (a solid shape). Next, liquid resin is added, which soaks into the cloth and then hardens. When the form is removed, the carbon fibre holds its shape. The part is lighter and stronger than if it was made of metal.

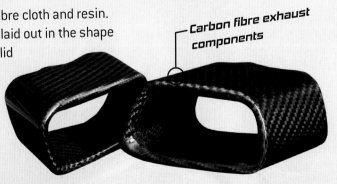

Carbon fibre exhaust components

LOTUS EXIGE CUP 430

Lotus is famous for valuing light weight. The company's founder, Colin Chapman, believed that less weight gave better results than more power.

ADJUSTABLE SUSPENSION

The rebound and compression of the suspension (how quickly it bounces up and down over bumps) can be switched between up to 24 different settings. This means the driver can tune the suspension to set the handling how he or she likes it.

RACING CAR ON THE ROAD

You can legally drive an Exige Cup on a road, but it's really designed for the racetrack. Almost everything possible has been stripped out. You can get carpets as an optional extra, but Lotus mostly prefers to leave them out. To make up for it, the Exige Cup does come with a lot of racetrack tools.

CHEAP THRILLS?

A basic Exige Cup costs about £100,000, as long as you don't go mad ordering extras like a stereo, or sound insulation so that you can hear the stereo. It goes from 0-100 kph in 3.3 seconds, which is:

⚙ 1.2 seconds faster than an Alfa Romeo 4C that costs half as much (but does look more attractive)

⚙ 0.4 seconds faster than a Jaguar F-Type SVR, which costs at least £10,000 more

⚙ the same as a Lamborghini Huracán, priced at £180,000 or more

⚙ only 0.7 seconds slower than a Pagani Zonda Revolución. The Zonda weighs the same (about 1070 kg), has a 5987 cc V12 engine and costs over £2 million.

The Exige Cup costs £80,000 less than this Lamborghini Huracán

> Adding power makes you faster in a straight line. Subtracting weight makes you faster everywhere.

Colin Chapman

ELECTRONIC CONTROLS

There are four electronic driver modes: Drive, Sport, Race and Off. In Off mode, the driver controls everything and must be skilful enough to drive very fast without crashing. The traction control can also be adjusted to allow the car to drift. There are five settings ranging from 1–12 per cent slip. Traction control can also be turned off.

PAGANI HUAYRA ROADSTER

Pagani was one of the first supercar makers to use carbon-fibre technology. Today it is famous for cars that are super-light, super-fast and use carbon fibre wherever possible.

The Huayra supercar has gullwing doors

GEARBOX

The driver changes gear using an 'automated manual' system. Pulling a paddle behind the steering wheel sends an electronic signal telling the gearbox to change. The system weighs a little over half as much as similar ones on other supercars.

FAMILY HISTORY

The Roadster is an open-topped version of the Huayra supercar – a car so fast that they named it after a South American wind god. Pagani originally made 100 Huayras, which quickly sold out, despite costing about £1 million. Then it made 20 Huayra BCs, a more powerful, more aerodynamic version that cost £2 million. All the cars were sold before they had even been built. Next came the Roadster.

CARBON-FIBRE MONOCOQUE

The car is built around a monocoque frame. Pagani makes this from materials it calls Carbo-Titanium and Carbo-Triax HP52. The monocoque is 52 per cent stiffer than the Huayra BC's, but the same weight.

ROADSTER CHALLENGE

Pagani describes the Roadster as "the most complicated project we have ever undertaken." The challenge was to make the car lighter than the Huayra BC, stiff enough to handle well and safe to drive. It took six years to make 100 cars; no wonder they cost £2,300,000 each. Even at that price they were all sold before they had been built.

LIGHTWEIGHT SUSPENSION

The Roadster has a suspension system made of lightweight aluminium. It weighs only three-quarters as much as the Huayra BC's suspension.

LAMBORGHINI CENTENARIO

100-YEAR BIRTHDAY

Centenario is Italian for 'hundredth birthday'. In 2016 it was 100 years since the birth of Ferruccio Lamborghini, who founded the company. Lamborghini decided to build a special car to celebrate. But how do you make a Lamborghini — already one of the most special cars in the world — even more special?

Lamborghinis are unmistakable. These are big, wide, low-down supercars, with hard edges to their design and a deafening noise coming out of the exhaust.

MAKE IT FASTER

To imagine how fast the Centenario is, try this: say: "One Mississsippi, two Mississippi, three Mississ—". Between the "One" and the final "Mississ—", the Centenario could hit 100 kph from a standing start. If you want to be exact, it takes 2.8 seconds.

> **When you mash on the throttle, the power is instant. It feels like you're going 200 miles an hour: it is insane.**
> Brian Roberts

SUPERCAR ★ SUPERSTAR

CAR: Lamborghini Centenario   **GAME:** 'Forza Horizon 3'

MOVIES: *Transformers: The Last Knight*

In *Transformers: The Last Knight*, a Centenario appears as the ride of Rodimus Prime – also known as 'Hot Rod'. Hot Rod's job is to save the world, so his car is important.

The Centenario was also on the cover of 'Forza Horizon 3' and was one of the game-play cars. The game appeared before the Centenario was released, so gamers got to (virtually) drive one before any real-life owners.

MAKE IT LIGHTER

The Centenario is built around a carbon-fibre monocoque and every possible body panel is also carbon fibre. Even the steering wheel and door mirrors are carbon fibre to save weight.

MAKE IT EXCLUSIVE

Lamborghini only made 40 Centenarios: 20 hard-top coupes and 20 open-top roadsters. If you're thinking about which to get, you might like to know that the Roadster is 0.1 seconds slower to 100 kph.

FOUR-WHEEL STEERING

The Centenario has all-wheel steering. The car combines four-wheel drive with a steering system that turns the rear wheels as well as the front ones. The result is faster, smoother steering and increased grip.

9FF PORSCHE GTURBO

The GTurbo is built in Germany by the car tuning company 9ff. It's based on the Porsche GT3, a £112,000 supercar that weighs 1,413 kg. The GTurbo weighs 1,210 kg – an amazing 14 per cent less.

SUPERCAR ★ SUPERSTAR

CAR: Porsche 911

MOVIE: Atomic Blonde

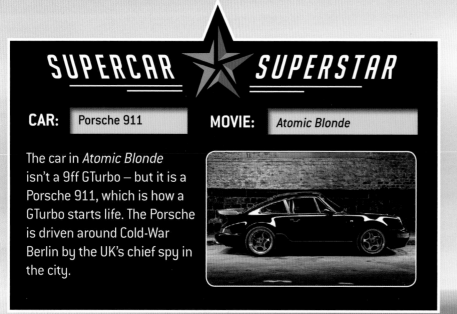

The car in *Atomic Blonde* isn't a 9ff GTurbo – but it is a Porsche 911, which is how a GTurbo starts life. The Porsche is driven around Cold-War Berlin by the UK's chief spy in the city.

TURBO POWER

9ff work to make the car more powerful. The company adds turbochargers to the non-turbo GT3. Power jumps from 368 kW to anywhere between 552 kW and 882 kW (which is a massive 240 per cent increase).

TITANIUM EXHAUST

The GTurbo's exhaust is partly made of titanium, a metal as strong as aluminium but lighter, to save weight. Some engine parts have also been made with titanium.

HEAD-TO-HEAD

The GTurbo is not only lighter than the GT3, it's also faster. Different engines are available, but if you buy the most powerful version, it's a LOT faster than a GT3:

	GT3	GTurbo
0–100 kph:	3.4 sec	3.2 sec
0–200 kph:	10.6 sec	6.7 sec
0–300 kph:	37.1 sec	12.4 sec
Top speed:	320 kph	395 kph
Power:	368 kW	882 kW

" Of the thousands of cars I've driven in my career, this is probably the most outrageous. "

Motortrend magazine

STRIPPED DOWN

9ff puts the GT3 through what it calls 'extreme weight reduction'. They remove the inside lining everywhere except the front. Then they fit a carbon roof, lightweight aluminium doors and bonnet, and polycarbonate windows.

TUNED SPECIAL

The GTurbo is a tuned special. Tuning is when specialist companies (tuners) give a performance car even more performance by changing some of its parts. Tuners usually work on the engine, gearbox and exhaust to give a car more power. They change the suspension so it can cope with the extra power, and improve the car's handling.

SPEED AND ACCELERATION

You'll know by now that the two most important numbers for supercars are: top speed (a number supercar owners want to be as big as possible); and time to reach 100 kph (a number that should be as small as possible).

WORLD'S FASTEST SUPERCAR

After averaging 447.2 kph in a speed test in November 2017, the Koenigsegg Agera RS became the world's fastest supercar. At one point, the car reached 457.94 kph. In total 25 Agera RSs were built for sale, most of them specially customised (built exactly as the owner wanted).

Koenigsegg Agera RS

" This is a proper monster car. The noise is unbelievable! It's really hard to describe what this much grunt (power) feels like ... it is crazy. "

Car and Driver magazine

ENGINE SPEED

If two cyclists race each other on identical bikes, in the same gear, the winner will be the one who can pedal fastest. In a car engine, it's the speed at which the engine can turn the crankshaft that counts. This is measured in revolutions per minute (rpm). Cars with a higher maximum rpm can 'pedal' faster than cars with a lower rpm, so they are quicker in the same gear.

Cars are fitted with tachometers so the driver can monitor the engine's rpm.

TECH TOPIC: GEARING

A car's top speed and acceleration are affected by its gears and how quickly the engine can turn the crankshaft. The easiest way to think about these is to compare them to riding a bicycle.

If you start pedalling a bike in an 'easy' gear, it accelerates quickly but has a low top speed: your legs can't pedal fast enough to go fast in that gear.

If you start pedalling in a 'hard' gear, the bike accelerates more slowly but its top speed is higher.

Track cyclists in the team sprint, straining to get going at the start of the race.

EASY GEAR

accelerates faster   lower top speed

HARD GEAR

accelerates more slowly   higher top speed

HENNESSEY VENOM GT/F5

Hennessey is a small supercar maker from the USA. Until the Koenigsegg Agera RS came along, the Venom GT was the world's fastest car. Hennessey hopes the Venom F5 may take back the title.

VIPER + EXIGE = VENOM

The Venom was developed from a Hennessey car called a Viper. In 2007 the Viper was the world's fastest car to 321.4 kph (200 mph). Hennessey decided to put the powerful engine from a Viper into a super-light Lotus Exige (see page 40).

The result was the Venom. In 2014 this hit 435.2 kph — 4.1 kph faster than the previous supercar record holder, the Bugatti Veyron.

NEW BODY SHAPE

The F5 is the same height as the GT but longer and wider. This has improved the car's aerodynamics. The F5 has less air resistance, which helps it go faster than the GT.

VENOM F5

The Venom F5 first appeared in 2017 after four years of work. It shares its name with the Venom GT but is a new car. The F5 has one purpose in life: to go fast.

TOP-SPEED DISPUTE

Not everyone agrees that the Venom should be included in the list of supercar record holders. Its top speed was based on a single high-speed run. Record-breaking speeds are usually an average of two runs, done in opposite directions in case there is a slight slope to the test track. Also, only 13 were sold: many fewer than the 30 sales needed to qualify as a production car.

" A savage burst of cheek-smooshing, gut-compressing, momentarily brain-addling force, the strongest I've ever experienced in a road-going car. "

Douglas Kott

ENGINE IMPROVEMENTS

The F5's engine is 7400 cc, which is 400 cc bigger than the GT's. It has up to 1,190 kW of power, compared to the 1,082 kW of the most powerful version of the GT. The F5 also has a seven-speed semi-automatic gearbox, rather than the GT's six-speed manual.

LAMBORGHINI HURACÁN

LP 610-4 POLIZIA

Italy is where many of the world's most famous supercars are made and driven. All those supercars mean the Italian police really need one of their own, for chasing speeders. Say hello to the Huracán LP610-4 Polizia.

SUPERCAR COPS

Italian cops are used to having nice cars. They used to have three Lamborghini Gallardos, but one was destroyed in an accident. In 2014 the police got a Huracán Polizia (*polizia* is Italian for 'police') to replace it.

The Huracán Polizia is a 325 kph speed machine. It is powered by a 5200 cc, 455 kW, V10 engine. It's also the world's cheapest supercar, as it was a gift from Lamborghini. Today it is often seen in Emilia-Romagna, the part of Italy where Lamborghini, Ferrari, Pagani and the motorbike maker Ducati all have their factories.

SIRENS

Four different specially designed sirens are fitted to the Polizia. They have to be extra loud so that the noise they make can outrun the car. Otherwise drivers wouldn't hear the sirens in time to pull over.

ORGAN TRANSPORT

Inside the Polizia is a special refrigeration unit. This is sometimes used to store human organs: the car can make high-speed organ deliveries to hospitals.

GIVING CHASE

On board is a special computer called a 'proof video data system'. This can target a vehicle the Polizia is chasing and work out exactly how fast it's going. The system sends this information back to police headquarters.

LIGHTS

The police lights on top of the Polizia had to be custom-built. The car is so fast that normal lights would have flown off long before it reached top speed.

SUPERCAR ★ POLICE CAR

Italy is not the only country where some police officers drive supercars.

⚙ Dubai: the police here have at least one 350+ kph Aston Martin One-77.

⚙ In the West Midlands, UK, a Lotus Evora is used as a high-speed chase car.

⚙ Evoras have also been used by police in Italy and Romania.

⚙ The state police force in New South Wales, Australia, uses a Porsche Panamera.

A Lotus Evora used by the West Midlands Police.

POLICE

POLIZIA 113
www.poliziadistato.it

⏱ THE RING

'The Ring' is the nickname of a famous racetrack: the Nürburgring in Germany. Anyone can turn up, pay their money and race around as fast as their car/motorbike/truck/tour bus/motorhome will go.

TWO TRACKS

The Nürburgring is really two tracks. The older track is the Nordschleife, or 'north loop'. It's a crazy, 20.8 km loop of tarmac that twists and turns, rises and falls through a thick forest. In 1976, Ferrari Formula One driver Niki Lauda had a bad accident here and the track was declared too dangerous for Grand Prix races. Now, people pay to drive round it and there's a high-speed straight where supercar makers like to push their cars to top speed.

A new Grand Prix circuit was built in 1984. It has modern safety features, such as large run-off zones and gravel beds to slow cars that come off the track.

NORDSCHLEIFE
This longer section dates back to the 1920s. The highest part is more than 300 metres above the lowest point on the track.

High-speed straight

GP-STRECKE
This new, shorter track is used for all major and international racing events.

DRIVE THE RING

You can get some idea of what it's like to drive around the Ring on the nurburgringlaptimes.com website. It keeps a list of the 100 fastest laps ever done at the Ring, most with videos shot from the point of view of the driver or passenger. Check the list here: **nurburgringlaptimes.com/lap-times-top-100/**

RADICAL BY NAME

The Radical SR8 is one of the fastest cars ever around the Ring. In 2005 it became the first to complete the Nordschleife in under seven minutes, with a time of 6:56.08. Four years later a Radical SR8LM went even faster: 6:48.00. It took another seven years for a NIO EP9 to shave 2.1 seconds off this record.

SUPERCAR TESTING

Many supercar manufacturers test their cars at the Ring. The track is not always open to the public. Supercar makers are said to take their cars there when no one is looking. If the car sets a good time, they go back and do it again for everyone to see. For owners, being able to say their supercar did a lap of the Nordschleife in under seven minutes is a big deal.

All supercar companies employ professional test drivers. The most famous one is probably Valentino Balboni. He test drove every car Lamborghini developed for 40 years. He started as an apprentice mechanic in 1968, aged 19, and retired in 2008. He was so important to Lamborghini that they named a special version of the Gallardo supercar after him.

The Radical SR8LM

PORSCHE 918
SPYDER WEISSACH

In 2013, a 918 Spyder Weissach set a time of 6:57.00 at the Nürburgring. It became the fastest production car ever around the Nordschleife circuit.

HYBRID POWER

The 918 is a hybrid-power car, with a 4593 cc V8 petrol engine and two electric motors. Roughly two-thirds of the 918's power come from the petrol engine, the other third comes from the electric motors. In total they produce 652 kW of power and rocket the car to 100 kph in just 2.6 seconds.

ALL-WHEEL DRIVE

Power is fed to all four wheels. The suspension adapts to how the car is being driven and the track/road surface. This gives it excellent grip while accelerating, cornering and braking: just what you need on the Nordschleife.

SUPERCAR ⭐ SUPERSTAR

CAR:	Porsche 918 Spyder
MOVIE:	Nordschleife v. Porsche 918 Spyder

This is Porsche's video of parts of the 918's record-breaking lap of the Nordschleife (find it at https://www.porsche.com/657). The video shows how close to its limit the car is being driven.

> " The 918 is astonishing ... terrific grip and a willingness to change direction on the throttle. The brakes are sensational, too. "
>
> Autocar magazine

LIGHTWEIGHT

The biggest weight saving from the standard 918 is in the wheels. They're made of magnesium, saving 15 kg. The roof, rear wing and windscreen surround are all unpainted carbon (a layer of paint just might make a difference to the lap time).

WEISSACH EDITION

Massive power is only part of the reason for the 918's speed around the Nordschleife. The record-setting car was a special Weissach edition of the 918. This is lighter than the standard 918. Among the tiny changes made to lose weight were ceramic wheel bearings (-700 g), carbon shift paddles (-200 g) and leather-loop door openers instead of actual handles (-200 g). These may sound like tiny amounts, but they add up: the Weissach edition is 41 kg lighter.

LAMBORGHINI
HURACÁN PERFORMANTE

In 2017 the Porsche 918 Spyder lost its Nürburgring lap record – or did it? Within days of the video of the Huracán Performante's lap being released, some experts were questioning its new record time.

NUMBERS GAME

The Performante set a time of 6:52.01 around the Ring, five seconds faster than the 918 Spyder. Comparing the numbers for each car made some people ask how this was possible:

	918 Spyder	Huracán Performante
Engine	4593 cc non-turbo V8 2 x electric motors	5200 cc non-turbo V10
Power	653 kW	470 kW
Weight	1634 kg	1382 kg
0–100 kph	2.6 sec	2.9 sec
0–200 kph	7.2 sec	8.9 sec

The Spyder has a more powerful engine; each kW of power has to move less weight; and it's faster to 200 kph.

So how could the Performante be faster?

ACTIVE AERODYNAMICS

The record-breaking Huracán Performante was fitted with an active aerodynamic system. This adapts to driving conditions the whole time. At one extreme, it creates 750 per cent more downforce than a standard Huracán's. At the other, the car slips through the air with minimum drag.

AERODYNAMIC CORNERING

The aerodynamic system also helped the Huracán Performante go round corners faster. As the car cornered, the aerodynamics added extra downforce to the inside wheels (the ones closest to the inside of the bend). This meant the car didn't have to turn as hard so its cornering speed increased.

PROOF FROM LAMBORGHINI

To prove the record time was valid, Lamborghini released performance data from the Huracán Performante's lap. When experts analysed the car's speed in different parts of the racetrack, almost all agreed that the record-breaking time was accurate.

Lamborghini also revealed that the car's amazing lap time was because of its new aerodynamic system.

SPECIAL TYRES

To make the advantages of the aerodynamic system even greater, the Huracán Performante was fitted with special tyres. They were made by the manufacturer Pirelli specially for the record attempt.

DODGE VIPER
ACR EXTREME

The Nürburgring is a European track and few US car makers test their vehicles there. In 2017, though, a Dodge Viper ACR Extreme smashed its way into the top ten fastest cars ever around the Nordschleife circuit.

MUSCLE PLUS

High-powered American cars are sometimes called muscle cars. They were originally mass-produced two-door cars with powerful engines added. The suspension and aerodynamics could not always cope with the power of the engine so early ones could be tricky to drive. The Viper ACR Extreme is a muscle car plus, with advanced suspension and aerodynamics.

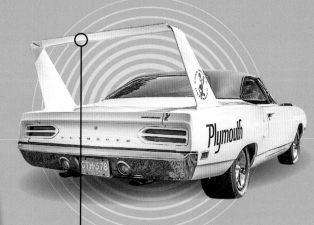

This Plymouth Roadrunner is an old-style muscle car. Even with its massive rear wing it was a handful to drive.

SUPER-STIFF SUSPENSION

To handle the aerodynamic, cornering and braking forces of the Nürburgring, the ACR Extreme had front suspension three times as stiff as a normal Viper's. The rear suspension was twice as stiff.

FULL POWER

At the heart of the Viper ACR Extreme was a huge 8382 cc V10 engine, which produced 481 kW of power. Even so, it's actually slower than a normal Viper. The car generates so much downforce and grip that it can only reach 285 kph, compared to the standard car's 332 kph.

EXTREME AERODYNAMICS

The car got its 'Extreme' name from its aerodynamics. At top speed the aerodynamic features push down with nearly 800 kg of downforce.

SUPERCAR ★ SUPERSTAR

CAR: Dodge Viper ACR Extreme

MOVIE: *The Last Viper*

In 2017, Dodge built the last V10 Viper. They invented a story about the last car for a video, which is available free on video-sharing sites. Search for 'the last viper' and it should appear.

The car in the video has the registration V8 EATR. A year or so later there must have been some red faces: the new Viper, due in 2021, is going to have a V8 engine.

TOP 10 AROUND THE RING

In mid-2018, these were the fastest 10 cars around the Nürburgring's Nordschleife track:

#	Car	Time
1	NIO EP9	6:45.90
2	Radical SR8LM	6:48.00
3	Lamborgini Huracán Performante	6:52.01
4	Radical SR8	6:56.08
5	Porsche 918 Spyder Weissach	6:57.00
6	Lamborghini Aventador LP 750-4	6:59.73
7	Viper ACR Extreme	7:01.30
8	Nissan GTR Nismo	7:08.68
9	Mercedes-AMG GT-R	7:10.92
10	Gumpert Apollo Speed	7:11.57

Mercedes-AMG GT-R

DO YOU SPEAK SUPERCAR?

Some of the words people use when they talk about supercars can be a bit confusing or hard to remember. Here's a reminder of some of the most common ones.

24-hour race: race on a racetrack, in which the winner is the team that drives furthest in 24 hours. Usually each car has three drivers, who take it in turns

body-on-frame construction: a way of building cars where the car parts and body are added to a strong base frame. Contrast this with **monocoque** construction

body panel: part of a car's outside 'skin', such as the outer part of a door

cc: short for cubic centimetres, a unit for measuring volume. cc and litres are the main ways to describe engine size

closed road: road on which normal traffic is not allowed

compression: in a car's suspension, compression describes two things: 1) the amount the suspension moves when it hits a bump; 2) the speed at which it moves (the full name for this is the 'compression rate')

configuration: in car engines, this is the word for how the engine's cylinders are arranged, for example as a flat four or a V8

crankshaft: a rotating shaft, usually made of metal, inside an engine. It is driven by the pistons inside the engine's cylinders

custom-built: specially made for a particular person or job

disc brake: brake that works by gripping a disc, usually made of metal, with two pads. The pads are pushed together by a caliper (a clamp that can squeeze and release)

downforce: downward pressure caused by the flow of air around a moving object

drag: force that acts in the opposite direction to a solid object (such as a car) moving through a fluid

drifting: sliding either the rear wheels or all four wheels of a car as you go around a bend

DRS: stands for Drag Reduction System. On the rear wing of a racing car, it is a part designed to move to reduce **drag**. There are rules which say when it can be activated by the driver in a race

eject: leave quickly and suddenly; in Bond films, either Bond or his enemies sometimes leave Bond's car by being ejected at high speed through the roof

form: a solid object that fabric can be wrapped around. The form makes the fabric take on the same shape as the outside of the form

Formula E: race series for electric-powered cars, held on the streets of some of the world's most famous cities

grip: ability to hold on to or stick to something

hillclimb: time trial in which cars take it in turns to try to reach the top of a hill in the fastest time

homologation: process of approving a car for use in a particular kind of racing

hybrid: vehicle that uses both a petrol engine and an electric motor

inside wheels: when a car goes around a corner, the wheels closest to the tightest part of the bend are called the inside wheels

kW: short for kilowatt, a unit of power often used for car engines. Another unit of power that is used for engines is bhp (brake horsepower: 1 kW = 1.4 bhp)

manual: gears that the driver changes using controls inside the car, usually a gearstick

monocoque: shell, usually of carbon fibre, around which the rest of a supercar is built

muscle car: not everyone agrees on exactly what makes a muscle car. Most are mass-produced two-door cars with powerful engines

optional extra: something you can have if you pay extra for it

POV: short for Point Of View. Most supercar videos are shot from the driver or passenger's POV

production car: according to the *Guinness Book of Records*, for a car to count as a production car at least 30 must have been sold

prototype: first or early version of something, made to test the design before more are built

rear-wheel drive: describes a vehicle with the engine's power going to the rear wheels

rebound: in a car's suspension, rebound describes two things: 1) the way the suspension moves the wheel away from the car; 2) the speed at which it moves (the proper name for this is the 'rebound rate')

resin: thick liquid that hardens as it cools or is exposed to sunlight

revs: short for revolutions, which is short for revolutions per minute: see **rpm**

roll bar: strong, curved bar behind the driver and passengers in an open-topped car, which stops them being crushed if the car rolls over

rpm: short for revolutions per minute. It describes how many times the engine can turn the crankshaft in 60 seconds

self-driving car: also known as an autonomous car or driverless car, this is a car that uses computers and sensors to drive itself

splitter: aerodynamic device usually at the front of a car, sticking out low down. The splitter channels air above and below the car at different speeds, adding downforce

standing start: starting from a motionless position; the car is stopped rather than already moving

stiff: not very flexible or easy to bend/move. Cars may be said to have stiff suspension, for example

suspension: a system including the car's tyres, springs and shock absorbers which absorbs bumps in the road surface to help the tyres grip the road better

telemetry: recording and then displaying data, for example speed, acceleration and braking force

torque: refers to the force making the wheels rotate, which pushes the driver back into the seat when he or she presses hard on the accelerator. It is measured in Newton metres

traction control: computerised system for helping a car grip the road better

tuner: person or company that changes parts on a car to improve its engine, aerodynamics, power or other aspects of performance

vane: blade-like shape that is used to control the way a solid object travels through a fluid

weight distribution: the way weight is spread out in a vehicle, such as a car, boat or aeroplane. In a car, it usually describes how much weight is carried by the front and rear wheels. For example, 45/55 weight distribution would mean 45 per cent of the weight was on the front wheels, 55 per cent on the rear ones

wind tunnel: large space with a giant fan at one end. The fan can pull air through at different speeds. Wind tunnels are used to test a car's aerodynamic performance

wing: wide, flat shape attached to the rear of a car to add downforce and grip. A wing is different from a spoiler, which is part of the car's actual body

---

ⓘ FINDING OUT MORE

Books to read

If you like to dig into the data:
Supercars series, by Paul Mason (Franklin Watts, 2017):
American Supercars, British Supercars, Italian Supercars, German Supercars

For a lot of fascinating information in a single book:
Top Marques: Supercars
by Rob Colson (Wayland, 2016)

A good reference book for classic and modern supercars:
Supercars: The World's Top Performance Machines
by Richard Gunn (Amber Books, 2017)

Places to visit

Haynes International Motor Museum
Sparkford, Yeovil, Somerset BA22 7LH
www.haynesmotormuseum.com

Jaguar Visitor Centre
Jaguar Land Rover, Lode Lane, Solihull,
West Midlands, B92 8NW
and Chester Road, Castle Vale, Birmingham, B35 7RA
www.jaguar.co.uk

Lotus Factory
Potash Lane, Hethel, Norwich, Norfolk NR14 8EZ
www.lotuscars.com

INDEX

QUOTE CREDITS

p5: Jeremy Clarkson [www.driving.co.uk/news clarkson-on-supercars/

p9: Andrew English, reviewing the Lamborghini Aventador S

p11: *Daily Telegraph* review of the Ferrari 812 Superfast

p15: LaFerrari Aperta review in *Car* magazine

p17: Nicki Shields, presenter of the Supercharged TV show

p23: Description of the Apollo IE on *motor1.com*

p27: Report on the FXX-K in *Evo* magazine

p33: Review of the Chiron in the *Sunday Times*

p41: Colin Chapman, founder of Lotus

p45: Brian Roberts reviews the Centenario for *Motorweek*

p47: Review of a 9ff GTurbo in *Motortrend* magazine

p48: Review of the Agera R [an earlier version of the RS for *Car and Driver* magazine

p51: Douglas Kott describes the acceleration of a Venom GT, in *Road and Track* magazine

p57: Review of the 918 Weissach in *Autocar* magazine